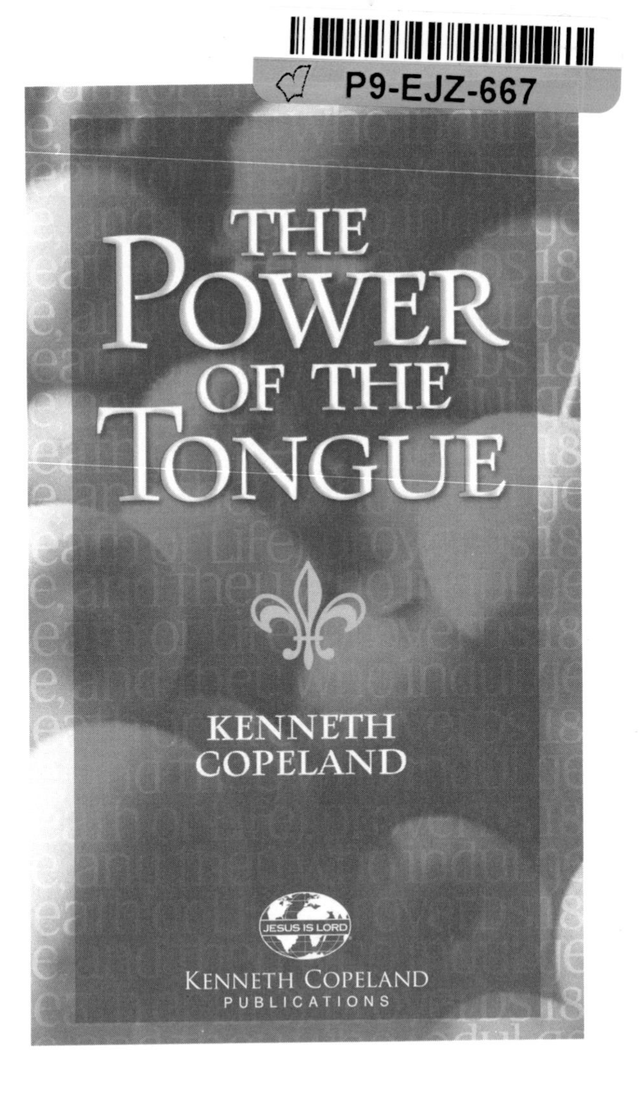
THE
POWER
OF THE
TONGUE
KENNETH
COPELAND
JESUS IS LORD
KENNETH COPELAND
PUBLICATIONS

Unless otherwise noted, all scripture is from the *King James Version* of the Bible.

The Power of the Tongue

ISBN-10 1-57562-113-4 30-0014
ISBN-13 978-1-57562-113-5

23 22 21 20 19 18 44 43 42 41 40 39

Kenneth Copeland Publications
Fort Worth, TX 76192-0001

For more information about Kenneth Copeland Ministries, visit kcm.org or call 1-800-600-7395 (U.S. only) or +1-817-852-6000.

The Power of the Tongue

"Death and life are in the power of the tongue, and they who indulge it shall eat the fruit of it [for death or life]" (Proverbs 18:21, *Amplified Bible, Classic Edition*).

There is a Bible secret of words. Words are spiritual; they carry power. The words we speak are of vital importance to our lives. Jesus said, "I say unto you, That every idle word that men shall speak, they shall give account thereof in the day of judgment. For by thy words thou shalt be justified, and by thy words thou shalt be condemned" (Matthew 12:36-37).

When God created the human race, He placed in us the special ability to choose our own words and speak them forth at will. That ability makes the human being different from all other creatures, even the angels. Angels can speak, but they speak only the words God tells them to speak; they act, but only by command of God.

Man's unique ability to choose and speak words has become a key factor in the development of the human race.

The Creative Power in Words

Words have played a vital role in life since the beginning of time. God used words when He created the heaven and the earth. "Through faith we understand that the worlds were framed by the word of God" (Hebrews 11:3). God *spoke* the worlds into existence, as evidenced in the first chapter of Genesis: "And God said, Let there be light: and there was light" (verse 3). The literal Hebrew says, "God said, 'Light, be'; and light was." All power in the natural, physical world came into being when God spoke those words.

> And God said, Let there be a firmament.
>
> And God said, Let the waters be gathered together.
>
> And God said, Let the earth bring forth grass.

The words, *And God said,* appear ten times in the first chapter of Genesis. To the natural mind, the repetition is almost monotonous, but through spiritual understanding, you will realize that the Holy Spirit had it written that way to stress how vital a part words played in Creation.

Each time God spoke, He released His faith—the creative power to bring His words to pass. He created all things by the power of His Word and, according to Hebrews 1:3, He is still upholding all things by the Word of His power.

God's words produce exactly what He says. His method of operation *never* changes. Once He speaks, His words will come to pass. Look again at Genesis 1, and notice these words: "God said...and it was so." When God speaks, power is released and things move!

God created the world and everything in it; then He said:

> Let us make man in our image, after our likeness: and let them have dominion over the fish of the sea, and over the fowl of the air, and over the cattle, and over all the earth, and over every

creeping thing that creepeth upon the earth. So God created man in his own image, in the image of God created he him; male and female created he them (verses 26-27).

The moment God said these words in verse 26 is the moment man became alive. Man was created from the faith-filled words of God—words of power, dominion and life. Those words came from the very insides of God where the dominion and authority lie, so all of the power that it took to have dominion over the earth was a part of man from the very beginning. Man was made out of that power.

Adam was created in God's class. He was made in the likeness of God and, consequently, had a free will.

Genesis 1:28 says, "And God blessed them." To bless means "say something good about." He blessed them, and "said unto them, Be fruitful, and multiply, and replenish the earth, and subdue it: and have dominion over the fish of the sea, and over the fowl of the air, and over every living thing that moveth upon the earth."

When God said, "Be fruitful...multiply... replenish...subdue...have dominion," He made a covenant with man. Man was created with power. Then God gave man authority to use that power by making a covenant with him, guaranteeing him dominion over this earth.

Man had total authority to rule as a god over every living creature on earth, and he was to rule by speaking words. His words would carry the power and anointing of God that was in him from the time he was first created.

Power Perverted

It was not until Satan entered the picture that the power of words was perverted to bring death and destruction.

Satan is not a god. He is a fallen angel. He is not in the God class. Consequently, there is no creative power in him.

As an angel of God, Satan (or Lucifer) was forbidden to act by his own will, but he chose to exalt himself over God. He tried to use the power of words against God when he said, "I will exalt my throne above the stars of God: I will sit also upon the mount of the congregation, in the sides of the north: I will ascend above the heights of the clouds: I will be like the most High" (Isaiah 14:13-14).

By choosing his own words, Satan broke a cardinal law in the spirit world. He violated the limits of his authority and chose to stand against God. He said, "I will be like the Most High. I will exalt my throne above the stars of God!" But God would not stand for it. He answered, "Yet thou shalt be brought down to hell, to the sides of the pit" (Isaiah 14:15).

At that point, their words clashed and God's Word—the word of a free Spirit, a Spirit with authority—reigned victoriously over the word of an angelic power. Immediately, Satan was expelled from heaven.

By using cunning and deception, Satan approached Adam and Eve in the Garden of Eden. In Genesis 3, we see how he very subtly used the words God had spoken to them as a challenge to their faith and obedience.

God had said, "Of every tree of the garden thou mayest freely eat: But of the tree of the knowledge of good and evil, thou shalt not eat of it: for in the day that thou eatest thereof thou shalt surely die" (Genesis 2:16-17). But Satan came in the form of a serpent and said to them, "Yea, hath God said...?" (Genesis 3:1). The *Amplified Bible, Classic Edition* translates it: "Can it really be that God has said...?"

First Timothy 2:14 says the woman was deceived, but the man was not.

Adam had his eyes wide open. He knew what he was doing when he disobeyed God's command and took the forbidden fruit. Through that disobedience, Satan was able to obtain authority in the earth. He became man's god, or as 2 Corinthians 4:4 calls him, "the god of this world."

Though he has no creative power of his own, Satan uses the creative power in man's words to manipulate the circumstances of the world. Everything he produces is only a counterfeit of the real. He takes what God has already created and perverts it to his own use.

James 3:6 tells us that the tongue is set on fire of hell. Satan desires the use of men's tongues. Tongues of creatures in the God class are much more powerful. Man was created in God's image.

God's Word Sent Forth

God places a high priority on words.

He has never done anything without saying it first, as we have seen from Genesis 1.

God's faith-filled Word was the original force in the universe. At creation, God set into motion what I call *the law of Genesis,* dictating that every living thing would produce after its own kind.

God's plan was for man to live eternally, producing a race that would be in close fellowship and communion with Him. But once Adam disobeyed God, that plan was altered. The authority that had been delegated to man was suddenly in the hands of Satan.

At that point, God was forced back to the original source—His Word. He couldn't make another man from the dust of the earth, because the ground was cursed. He had to revert to speaking His Word, filled with faith.

Immediately, God began to search for a man who would teach His children and live uprightly before Him. Finally, He found that man, Abram.

He made a covenant with Abram—a covenant that was to last forever. "As for me, behold, my covenant is with thee.... And I will make thee exceeding fruitful.... And I will establish my covenant between me and thee and thy seed after thee in their generations for an everlasting covenant, to be a God unto thee, and to thy seed after thee" (Genesis 17:4, 6-7).

Once that covenant was established, God began to release His Word into the earth. He began to paint a picture of a Redeemer, a man who would be the manifestation of His Word in the earth.

The only avenue God had to get His words into the earth was through men. As He would speak life-filled words in relation to His covenant with Abraham, His prophets would repeat those words in the earth. It was a very tedious and difficult process since the Old Testament prophets were not born-again men. Because they lived under the Abrahamic Covenant, they were able to receive instruction from God and righteousness was imputed, or counted, unto them (Romans 4:22).

So before Jesus came to the earth, God

spoke His Word and then spoke His Word again. How many times did He say the Messiah was coming? It was prophesied over hundreds, even thousands, of years. He kept saying, "He is coming. He is coming."

The circumstances in the earth made it look as if there was no way He could accomplish it, but He just kept saying it. He would not be moved by what He saw. Once that Word was received into the earth by a man, it was here to stay.

In Isaiah 55:11, God said, "So shall my word be that goeth forth out of my mouth: it shall not return unto me void, but it shall accomplish that which I please, and it shall prosper in the thing whereto I sent it." God would not relent. Through the mouths of His prophets, He kept sending His Word and sending His Word.

Finally, the great moment came when that Word was brought forth in human form: "And the Word was made flesh, and dwelt among us, (and we beheld his glory, the glory as of the only begotten of the Father,) full of grace and truth" (John 1:14).

The Word, which existed before the foundation of the earth, lived for thirty-three years as a man. His Name was Jesus. He ministered for three years as a prophet under the Abrahamic Covenant. Then He gave Himself to be the last sacrifice of the Old Covenant. He became the sacrificial lamb, offered upon the altar of the Cross for one reason: to defeat Satan.

Jesus was the last Adam (1 Corinthians 15:45), and He passed the test that the first Adam failed. He paid the price for Adam's transgression. He took Adam's punishment, his sinfulness, his sickness and disease, his infirmities and his shame. Jesus bore all of this just as if He Himself had committed treason against God.

Jesus defeated Satan by going to the cross, dying a horrible death, and spending three days and nights in the heart of the earth, hell itself (Matthew 12:40). Acts 2 says Jesus was raised up, loosed from the *pains* of death (verse 24). Jesus is called the firstborn from the dead (Colossians 1:18). He was the first man to be born again from death to life. When He appeared to John on the Isle of Patmos, He said, "Fear not; I am the first and the last: I am he that liveth, and was dead; and, behold, I am alive for evermore, Amen; and have the keys of hell and of death" (Revelation 1:17-18).

Jesus defeated Satan in awful combat in full view of all Satan's cohorts. He took from Satan the keys of hell. He took back the authority that Satan had stolen from Adam in the Garden of Eden. He made an open show of principalities and powers, lording it over them in their own domain (Colossians 2:15).

Our Authority as Believers

Satan is still "the god of this world" (2 Corinthians 4:4) and he has authority in the earth over natural men, but Jesus has provided His Body of believers with the power and authority to overcome Satan in this world. We are not of this world, so Satan is not our god! In Matthew 28:18-19, Jesus said, "All power is given unto me in heaven and in earth. Go ye therefore...."

Mark 16:15-18 gives every believer that authority to stand against Satan. It is our responsibility to bind his forces and render him helpless. Through Jesus, we have been delivered out of the power of darkness and have been translated into the kingdom of God (Colossians 1:13), but we have to stand our ground to keep Satan from robbing us of our victory.

We are to execute judgment over Satan's kingdom. First Peter 5:8-9 says, "...Your adversary the devil, as a roaring lion, walketh about, seeking whom he may devour: whom resist stedfast in the faith."

The Weapons of Our Warfare

Jesus paid an awesome price so that we, as believers in Him, could be free from satanic influence. To live free, we have been given weapons. According to 2 Corinthians 10:4, "the weapons of our warfare are not carnal, but mighty through God to the pulling down of strong holds.)"

The basis of all our weapons is "the sword of the Spirit, which is the word of God" (Ephesians 6:17). Jesus is the living Word—the Word of God manifest in the flesh. Then God provided the written Word, the gospel, for us to use in our spiritual combat with Satan.

In Revelation 1:16, the Apostle John

describes his vision on the Isle of Patmos. He saw Jesus as having a sharp two-edged sword coming out His mouth. *That sword—the all-powerful and mighty Word of God—is ours to use in defense of our rights as born-again children of God.* According to Hebrews 4:12, The *Amplified Bible, Classic Edition,* the Word is alive and full of power, sharper than any two-edged sword, for the penetrating and dividing of soul and spirit, joints and marrow.

Our weapons are much more powerful than the weapons of Satan; but to be effective against him, we must learn our weapons and know how they function. In combat training, a soldier is drilled so thoroughly that he can take his rifle apart and put it back together in the dark, if necessary. That is how every believer should be trained in the Word of God.

But we must do more than just learn our weapons, we must be ready and willing to use them. A soldier's rifle is of no value to him if he doesn't use it. In spiritual combat today, many Christians are foolishly trying to fight without a true knowledge of God's Word. Even some, who know the Word, mistakenly wait until the last minute before taking their stand.

Several years ago, the Spirit of God taught me a valuable lesson in this area. As I was praying about my meetings, the Lord showed me that I had been trying to fight the battle after the enemy had swarmed over my position. I had been waiting until the meeting began to pray for its success.

I should have been interceding for the people weeks in advance, getting the stage set spiritually before I ever started the meeting. But I had been taking one day at a time. As Satan would come against me in one area, I would fight him there. Then he would attack in another area. He kept me tied up constantly, fighting little battles here and there. By waiting, I was giving Satan time to build up his fortresses before I would try to combat him, and consequently, I was losing almost every battle.

Then the Lord said something to me that I will never forget. He said, *If they had kicked Al Capone out of Chicago when he was just a small-time operator, he would not have been so hard to handle. But they waited until he became a first-class criminal with his forces built up around him. Then it took an army to bring him down.*

I learned my lesson well. Today, we pray and intercede for our meetings several weeks or months in advance, and when I begin a meeting, I can confidently say, "Father, in Jesus' Name, I roll all the care of this meeting over on You."

Exercising Authority

Satan will challenge you as much as he can to test your willingness to stand your ground. But by understanding and exercising your authority as a believer, you will always be able to triumph over him.

An outstanding example of the use of authority is a police officer. He wears a badge to show his authority and carries a weapon to reinforce that authority. Every policeman has the right to use his weapon in behalf of the law. In order to avoid the authority of the law, a criminal knows he has to avoid that weapon. If he can get around the pistol, he can get around the law.

Satan operates in much the same way. In order to maneuver around God, he has to avoid God's Word because the Word of God is where the power lies.

As a born-again believer, you are equipped with the Word. You have the power of God at your disposal. By getting the Word deep into your spirit and speaking it boldly out your mouth, you release spiritual power to change things in the natural circumstances of your life.

Jesus possessed authority in the earth, and He exercised that authority by the use of words. When He was in the midst of a storm at sea, He spoke the words, "Peace, be still," and the forces of the atmosphere were quick to obey (Mark 4:35-41). He knew spiritual law and He knew His enemy, Satan. He allowed neither one to stand in the way of what He was called to do.

The Power of Jesus' Words

In James 3, there is some powerful teaching with regard to the tongue and the power it contains. The Apostle James was Jesus' half brother. They were raised together in the same household. He saw Jesus deal with day-to-day situations.

Even though Jesus did not perform any miracles until He was thirty years old, He lived by faith all His life. Hebrews 11:6 says that without faith, it is impossible to please God, and Jesus certainly pleased God. Luke 2:40, speaking of Jesus, says, "And the child grew, and waxed strong in spirit, filled with wisdom: and the grace of God was upon him." Luke 2:52 says, "And Jesus increased in wisdom and stature, and in favour with God and man."

Jesus lived by faith from the time He had mental knowledge of how to use His own physical body. Because a person cannot live faith without talking faith, Jesus talked faith as well. His mother realized that about Him. She knew that whatever He said would come to pass. At the wedding feast at Cana, she said to the servants, "Whatever He says to you, do it" (John 2:5).

Everything Jesus did, everything He said, was completely contrary to the world's way. According to Mark 3:21, *Amplified Bible, Classic Edition,* Jesus' own kinsmen thought He was mentally deranged. They could not understand the ways of a man who walked and talked totally by faith. Even James, Jesus' half brother, was not able to understand until he himself had been born again and had the Holy Spirit within to teach him spiritual things.

The Tongue—A Little Member

James' Epistle to the Church reveals some of the things he saw in Jesus. His words are vital to our understanding of the power of the tongue. I want you to read this entire third chapter of James very closely.

> My brethren, be not many masters, knowing that we shall receive the greater condemnation. For in many things we offend all. If any man offend not in word, the same is a perfect man, and able also to bridle the whole body. Behold, we put bits in the horses' mouths, that they may obey us; and we turn about their whole body. Behold also the ships, which though they be so great, and are driven of fierce winds, yet are they turned about with a very small helm, whithersoever the governor listeth. Even so the tongue is a little member, and boasteth great

things. Behold, how great a matter a little fire kindleth! And the tongue is a fire, a world of iniquity: so is the tongue among our members, that it defileth the whole body, and setteth on fire the course of nature; and it is set on fire of hell. For every kind of beasts, and of birds, and of serpents, and of things in the sea, is tamed, and hath been tamed of mankind: But the tongue can no man tame; it is an unruly evil, full of deadly poison. Therewith bless we God, even the Father; and therewith curse we men, which are made after the similitude of God. Out of the same mouth proceedeth blessing and cursing. My brethren, these things ought not so to be. Doth a fountain send forth at the same place sweet water and bitter? Can the fig tree, my brethren, bear olive berries? either a vine, figs? so can no fountain both yield salt water and fresh. Who is a wise man and endued with knowledge among you? let him show out of a good conversation his works with meekness of wisdom. But if you

> have bitter envying and strife in your hearts, glory not, and lie not against the truth. This wisdom descendeth not from above, but is earthly, sensual, devilish. For where envying and strife is, there is confusion and every evil work. But the wisdom that is from above is first pure, then peaceable, gentle, and easy to be entreated, full of mercy and good fruits, without partiality, and without hypocrisy. And the fruit of righteousness is sown in peace of them that make peace.

In this chapter, there are two central ideas that I want us to pay particular attention to:

> 1. There is nothing in this earth so great or so powerful, including the physical body, that it cannot be controlled by the tongue.
>
> 2. The entire course of nature and the circumstances surrounding every human being are controlled by *that* person's tongue.

In verses 3-5, James uses some examples to illustrate:

> Behold, we put bits in the horses' mouths, that they may obey us; and we turn about their whole body. Behold also the ships, which though they be so great, and are driven of fierce winds, yet are they turned about with a very small helm whithersoever the governor listeth. Even so the tongue is a little member, and boasteth great things. Behold, how great a matter a little fire kindleth!

No matter how big or strong a horse may be, he can be controlled by a small piece of iron in his mouth. No matter what size a ship or how fierce the winds are against it, it can be directed by the helm, or rudder.

The parallel drawn between a ship's rudder, a bit in a horse's mouth and the human tongue is outstanding. They seem insignificant in themselves, but the power each wields is remarkable.

You are the rider holding the bridle—you

control the horse.

You are the governor, or captain, of the ship—you turn the rudder.

In either situation, you are in authority as long as you maintain control.

Your tongue is the deciding factor in your life. No mater how fierce the storm or how serious the problem, your tongue will turn it. No storm is so big that you, as a believer, cannot overcome it with God's Word in your mouth. Your confession will control your ship in the storm.

The Tongue Is a Fire

In verse 5, James makes a comparison between the tongue and kindling for a fire. He says, "Behold, how great a matter a little fire kindleth!" The tongue is to your circumstances what kindling is to a fire. Kindling is where the fire starts. A huge bonfire is begun by only a tiny piece of kindling. You can't start a fire with a big log. It won't burn. You have to begin with tiny bits and pieces of wood to use as kindling. When you set the kindling on fire, it in turn will cause the log to burn.

This is how the circumstances of our planet function. Satan is not powerful enough to start a bonfire with the big logs of this planet. *He has to begin with kindling, and the human tongue is the kindling he uses.*

Because he is a fallen angel with no creative power of his own, *he has to use the power delegated to man and manipulate that power to his own advantage.* Without the use of a person's tongue, he cannot function in the world, but when he has control of the tongue, he can control the entire realm of that person's life.

Words Are the Key

Verse 6 gives us the key to Satan's entire operation:

"And the tongue is a fire, a world of iniquity: so is the tongue among our members, that it defileth the whole body, and setteth on fire the course of nature; and it is set on fire of hell."

In the natural world, the tongue works like a fire, setting the entire course of life. By using the tongue, Satan controls the circumstances of life. First, he plants evil, negative thoughts into the mind. Then as they are dwelt upon, they drop down into the spirit; and finally, out of the abundance of the heart, the mouth will speak.

I want you to notice Jesus' words in Matthew 6:31: "Therefore take no thought, saying, What shall we eat? or, What shall we drink? or, Wherewithal shall we be clothed?" First, you *take* the thought, then you *say* it. That is how Satan operates in your life. It is not what you say only once, but what you say over and over. The thought is spoken into your spirit until it is in there in abundance. Then the same words will come out of your spirit through your mouth without your mind having to call for them. Those are the words that are filled with either faith or fear, love or hate—whatever thoughts you have been speaking.

By speaking negative thoughts, tiny flames are ignited. If not stopped, the little fires that were begun with the tongue will erupt into a huge bonfire to consume and destroy.

Every circumstance—the entire course of nature—is started with the tongue. Remember, death and life are in the power of the tongue, and they that indulge it will eat the fruit of it. The fruit of your mouth—whether good or evil, blessing or cursing—will manifest itself in your life. Jesus said it is not what goes into a man that defiles him; it is what comes out his mouth (Matthew 15:11, 18).

You have been trained since birth to speak negative, death-dealing words. Unconsciously in your everyday conversation, you use the words of death, sickness, lack, fear, doubt and unbelief: *That scared me to death. That tickled me to death. I laughed until I thought I would die. I'm just dying to go. That makes me sick. I'm sick and tired of this mess. I believe I'm taking the flu. We just can't afford it. I doubt it.*

Particularly in the area of finances, people question why God is not blessing them, when all the time it is His desire to do so. Through the words of their own mouths, they hinder His operation in their lives. They say, "God could never get me anything. He wouldn't give me anything. Who would ever give to me?" Their words become stout against God (Malachi 3:13).

You say these things without even realizing it. When you do, you set in motion negative forces in your life and the fire blazes. Now you can understand why James 3:10-12 says:

"Out of the same mouth proceedeth blessing and cursing. My brethren, these things ought not so to be. Doth a fountain send forth at the same place sweet water and bitter? Can the fig tree, my brethren, bear olive berries? either a vine, figs? so can no fountain both yield salt water and fresh."

Speaking the Word in Faith

So how do I put out the fire? With the washing of water by the Word (Ephesians 5:26).

Get the Word of God down deep into your spirit man. Jesus said, "Out of the abundance of the heart the mouth speaketh" (Matthew 12:34). When the Word is in your heart in abundance, it *will* come out your mouth. By speaking God's Word, you replace the negative forces at work in your life with the positive forces from the good treasure of your heart.

Just as your words loosed the power of

Satan, so can your words loose the power of God. Your words brought death and sickness; God's Word in your mouth will bring life and healing. Your words produced poverty and lack; God's Word will produce prosperity and abundance.

The spiritual principle of Mark 11:23 is basic to your life as a born-again believer. That is how God uses His faith. Jesus Himself said, "Have faith in God" (verse 22), or as the cross-reference says, "Have the faith of God." Then He continued to explain how the faith of God works. Notice the close connection between confessing with the mouth and believing with the heart.

"Whosoever shall *say* unto this mountain, Be thou removed, and be thou cast into the sea; and shall not doubt in his heart, but shall believe that those things which he *saith* shall come to pass; he shall have whatsoever he *saith.*"

Your own salvation was based on words. Romans 10:9-10 says, "If thou shalt confess with thy mouth the Lord Jesus, and shalt believe in thine heart that God hath raised him from the dead, thou shalt be saved. For with the heart man believeth unto righteousness; and with the mouth confession is made unto salvation."

Remember Jesus' words in Matthew 12:36-37: "But I say unto you, That every idle word that men shall speak, they shall give account thereof in the day of judgment. For by thy words thou shalt be justified, and by thy words thou shalt be condemned."

You are not justified by how much fasting you do or by how many hours you spend in prayer. Jesus said you are either justified or condemned by the words that come out your mouth. There is quite a price placed on words.

Stopping Satan With Words

Satan's number one ploy is to keep your attention on the experiences of life. He will keep you trying to analyze what happened to you and why. He will try to sell you the lie so many religious people have bought—that the storms of life come on you to teach you. As long as you believe that, Satan can keep you involved in those storms and see to it that you never live the victorious life.

Satan will say to you: *You're not going to make it.* If you agree with him, he will run roughshod over you. He will push you as far as he can. But I want you to realize that Satan can be stopped.

In Jesus' teaching from Matthew 6:31, He said, "Therefore take no thought, saying, What shall we eat? or, What shall we drink? or, Wherewithal shall we be clothed?" First, we take a thought; then we say it. By using this principle, you can stop Satan.

Take the thought, then say, "No, Satan, the Word of God says I have authority over you. I don't have to listen to you. I've been made the righteousness of God through Jesus Christ and I refuse to go one step further under your influence. I will not allow you to put sickness and disease on my body any longer. You are not my god. Jesus is my Lord."

Once you make that decision and speak forth the Word of God, you must be willing to hold your ground and not change or relent in any way. Satan will challenge you, so you will have to stand firm in his face and refuse to budge one inch!

By preaching this way, I have been accused of being too hard, but I have learned that to go easy on people would be doing them an injustice. Sometimes it takes being firm with people to jar their thinking and make them aware of how Satan is beating them down.

When the Syrophenician woman came to Jesus, it sounded as though He was being cruel to her when He said, "You don't take the children's bread and cast it to the dogs." His words were stout, but they penetrated her unbelief. When she began to believe God, Jesus said, "Be it unto thee even as thou wilt" (Matthew 15:22-28).

Words carry power. They convey either life or death, blessing or cursing. Have you ever stopped to think why it is so repulsive to hear people use God's name in vain? Why is it vain to say that God "damns"? Because God is not the damner. He is not the destroyer. He is the Creator.

Most people who hear someone using God's name in vain are repulsed by it. But then those very same people will turn around and blame God for all kinds of terrible things: *God took my baby from me. God killed my father. God caused a tornado to destroy my crops and kill my cattle.*

To accuse God of killing or destroying is the same as saying God "damns." God is love. He is life. He creates and brings forth good things. By saying that God caused death or destruction, you license Satan to condemn and destroy. Satan does the work and God gets the blame for it!

In our insurance policies, we use the phrase, "an act of God," when referring to fires, floods, earthquakes, tornadoes, etc. It is just as vain to say that God brought damnation on Southern California with an earthquake as it is to say that God "damns." The Word says in James 1:13, "Let no man say when he is tempted [tested or tried], I am tempted of God: for God cannot be tempted with evil, neither tempteth he any man."

In our thinking, we have classified certain words and phrases as being profane. But what is profanity? In God's eyes, profanity is anything crosswise to His Word, His nature, His

Name, His power or His love.

God is love. He is not sickness, disease, damnation or destruction. Jesus said, "The thief cometh not, but for to steal, and to kill, and to destroy: I am come that they might have life, and that they might have it more abundantly" (John 10:10).

The abundant life is being freely offered. However, many Christians are not living it because of ignorance. "My people are destroyed for lack of knowledge" (Hosea 4:6). Once you learn how the system works, then you can see how Satan has been manipulating it for his own cause.

"And the tongue is a fire, a world of iniquity...and [it] setteth on fire the course of nature; and it is set on fire of hell" (James 3:6). This is how the system works. Satan is using your tongue to set on fire the course of nature against you. From the moment you were born into the world, you were trained to speak negatively about your life and the circumstances around you. By using your tongue, Satan sets in motion the course of nature in your life.

Stop and listen to your everyday

conversation. Train yourself to hear your own words. Much of it is so-called "casual" remarks that you make, never thinking of the effect those words are having on your life.

For instance, when cold weather first sets in, there is much talk about the flu season being just around the corner. People comment to friends about the extra doctor bills they will have to pay. This kind of remark is a product of fear—fear that sickness and disease is coming, that it is inevitable.

If asked, "Do you believe in healing?" you answer, "Yes, of course," but your everyday conversation may negate that statement of faith. Proverbs 6:2 says you are snared with the words of your mouth.

As you make statements of fear, doubt, unbelief, etc., the pilot light of destruction is lit, and Satan will fan the flame every way he can to make it grow. Then once he gets that fire built up around you, he will attack. To your untrained eye, it will seem that tragedy struck from out of nowhere. The first thing you do is question, "Why? Why did this happen to me?" It seems to be an unanswerable question, but there is an answer: The tongue sets on fire the course of nature, and the tongue is set on fire by hell itself.

By knowing that your tongue controls the entire course of your life, you can put a stop to Satan's operation. *You can control Satan by learning to control your own tongue.* Though it may seem impossible, it can be done; but it requires the power of the Holy Spirit at work in your life.

James 3:7-8 says, "For every kind of beasts, and of birds, and of serpents, and of things in the sea, is tamed, and hath been tamed of mankind: but the tongue can no man tame; it is an unruly evil, full of deadly poison." Man can tame the wild beasts, but he cannot tame his own tongue.

This does not say that the tongue cannot be tamed. It simply says that *man* cannot tame it. The tongue cannot be tamed with the same natural power that man uses to tame the animals. It takes spiritual power, and spiritual power is what every born-again believer has at his disposal. Jesus said, "My words are spirit" (John 6:63). Thank God for His written Word!

Your tongue is only an instrument. Your heart is where the key lies. Whatever is in your heart in abundance is what will come out your mouth. If you fill your heart with God's Word, then God's Word will come out your mouth. You can begin today setting a new standard for your life by changing the words that come out your mouth. But first, you need to use the authority of God's Word and break the power of past words spoken.

I have prepared a confession of God's Word for you to use as your spiritual weapon. Take it and use it. Quench the fire that Satan has been building in your life. Put the fire out...now!

Thank God, you have the Word of God, the power of the Holy Spirit and the Name of Jesus. You have Jesus' advocate ministry to call upon from the book of 1 John: "If we confess our sins, he is faithful and just to forgive us our sins, and to cleanse us from all unrighteousness...And if any man sin, we have an advocate with the Father, Jesus Christ the righteous" (1 John 1:9, 2:1).

How did you receive Jesus as your Lord? By confessing it. How do you get sin out of your life? By confessing it. You speak that sin with your mouth and push it away from you. Revelation 12:11 says, "And they overcame him by the blood of the Lamb, and by the word of their testimony."

God will back His Word with His power. Put God's Word in your heart and it will come out your mouth. Your mouth has no choice. It will speak what is in your heart in abundance. Start today to build a brand new future by yielding your tongue to Jesus and His Word!

Father, in the Name of Jesus, I make the quality decision to take control of my tongue.

I renounce, reject and repent of every word I have spoken against You and Your operation in my life. I cancel the power of those words and dedicate my mouth to speaking Your Word.

Out of the abundance of the heart, the mouth speaks, so I set myself to fill my heart with Your Word. Put a watch, oh Lord, over my lips.

I set myself to speak in line with the Word. As Your child, I confess that I am healed, I am filled with Your mighty Holy Spirit, I am the righteousness of God though Jesus Christ. I am victorious in every area of my life, because You have made it so.

Father, I thank You that I no longer will be double-minded by the words of my mouth. I let the Word of Christ dwell in me richly in all wisdom. Everything I do, whether in word or deed, I do in the Name of the Lord Jesus Christ, giving thanks unto You.

In Jesus' Name,

Amen.

Prayer for Salvation and Baptism in the Holy Spirit

Heavenly Father, I come to You in the Name of Jesus. Your Word says, "Whosoever shall call on the name of the Lord shall be saved" (Acts 2:21). I am calling on You. I pray and ask Jesus to come into my heart and be Lord over my life according to Romans 10:9-10: "If thou shalt confess with thy mouth the Lord Jesus, and shalt believe in thine heart that God hath raised him from the dead, thou shalt be saved. For with the heart man believeth unto righteousness; and with the mouth confession is made unto salvation." I do that now. I confess that Jesus is Lord, and I believe in my heart that God raised Him from the dead. I repent of sin. I renounce it. I renounce the devil and everything he stands for. Jesus is my Lord.

I am now reborn! I am a Christian—a child of Almighty God! I am saved! You also said in Your Word, "If ye then, being evil, know how to give good gifts unto your children: HOW MUCH MORE shall your heavenly Father give the Holy Spirit to them that ask him?" (Luke 11:13). I'm also asking You to fill me with the Holy Spirit. Holy Spirit, rise up within me as I praise God. I fully expect to speak with other tongues as You give me the utterance (Acts 2:4). In Jesus' Name. Amen!

Begin to praise God for filling you with the Holy Spirit. Speak those words and syllables you receive—not in your own language, but the language given to you by the Holy Spirit. You have to use your own voice. God will not force you to speak. Don't be concerned with how it sounds. It is a heavenly language!

Continue with the blessing God has given you and pray in the spirit every day.

You are a born-again, Spirit-filled believer. You'll never be the same!

Find a good church that boldly preaches God's Word and obeys it. Become part of a church family who will love and care for you as you love and care for them.

We need to be connected to each other. It increases our strength in God. It's God's plan for us.

Make it a habit to watch the Believer's Voice of Victory Network and become a doer of the Word, who is blessed in his doing (James 1:22-25).

About the Author

Kenneth Copeland is co-founder and president of Kenneth Copeland Ministries in Fort Worth, Texas, and best-selling author of books that include *Honor—Walking in Honesty, Truth and Integrity,* and *THE BLESSING of The LORD Makes Rich and He Adds No Sorrow With It.*

Since 1967, Kenneth has been a minister of the gospel of Christ and teacher of God's WORD. He is also the artist on award-winning albums such as his Grammy-nominated *Only the Redeemed, In His Presence, He Is Jehovah, Just a Closer Walk* and *Big Band Gospel.* He also co-stars as the character Wichita Slim in the children's adventure videos *The Gunslinger, Covenant Rider* and the movie *The Treasure of Eagle Mountain,* and as Daniel Lyon in the Commander Kellie and the Superkids$_{TM}$ videos *Armor of Light* and *Judgment: The Trial of Commander Kellie.* Kenneth also co-stars as a Hispanic godfather in the 2009 and 2016 movies *The Rally* and *The Rally 2: Breaking the Curse.*

With the help of offices and staff in the United States, Canada, England, Australia, South Africa, Ukraine and Latin America Kenneth is fulfilling his vision to boldly preach the uncompromised WORD of God from the top of this world, to the bottom, and all the way around. His ministry reaches millions of people worldwide through daily and Sunday TV broadcasts, magazines, teaching audios and videos, conventions and campaigns, and the World Wide Web.

Learn more about Kenneth Copeland Ministries by visiting our website at **kcm.org**

We're Here for You!®

Your growth in God's WORD and victory in Jesus are at the very center of our hearts. In every way God has equipped us, we will help you deal with the issues facing you, so you can be the **victorious overcomer** He has planned for you to be.

The mission of Kenneth Copeland Ministries is about all of us growing and going together. Our prayer is that you will take full advantage of all The LORD has given us to share with you.

Wherever you are in the world, you can watch the *Believer's Voice of Victory* broadcast on television (check your local listings), the Internet at kcm.org or on our digital Roku channel.

Our website, **kcm.org,** gives you access to every resource we've developed for your victory. And, you can find contact information for our international offices in Africa, Australia, Canada, Europe, Ukraine and our headquarters in the United States.

Each office is staffed with devoted men and women, ready to serve and pray with you. You can contact the worldwide office nearest you for assistance, and you can call us for prayer at our U.S. number, +1-817-852-6000, seven days a week!

We encourage you to connect with us often and let us be part of your everyday walk of faith!

Jesus Is LORD!

Kenneth and Gloria Copeland